Omar Khayyam Poems

Omar Khayyam Poems

A Modern Translation

OMAR KHAYYAM

Translated by Siamak Akhavan

RESOURCE *Publications* • Eugene, Oregon

OMAR KHAYYAM POEMS
A Modern Translation

Copyright © 2021 Siamak Akhavan. All rights reserved. Except for brief quotations in critical publications or reviews, no part of this book may be reproduced in any manner without prior written permission from the publisher. Write: Permissions, Wipf and Stock Publishers, 199 W. 8th Ave., Suite 3, Eugene, OR 97401.

Resource Publications
An Imprint of Wipf and Stock Publishers
199 W. 8th Ave., Suite 3
Eugene, OR 97401

www.wipfandstock.com

PAPERBACK ISBN: 978-1-6667-1550-7
HARDCOVER ISBN: 978-1-6667-1551-4
EBOOK ISBN: 978-1-6667-1552-1

07/01/21

For all those that seek **Light** amidst the darkness.

With best wishes for that ever-lasting land of literature, poetry, and wisdom, Persia/Iran.

This is a non-profit project for the author, and all author proceeds from the sale of this book will be dedicated to cultural and educational programs in Iran.

Contents

Preface | ix
Introduction | xi
Poems | 1

Preface

THE POEMS ATTRIBUTED TO Omar Khayyam have a universal and timeless philosophical theme: life, even if brief and uncertain, is a meaningful journey. They inspire an unconstrained free-thinking mindset, a wise realization that guides thinking persons: it is impossible to see the absolute truth, for the universe has its own reality that remains largely hidden from us, and that one must think and act accordingly.

Khayyam, the 11th century scholar, mathematician and scientist, was not famed for his poetry by his contemporaries. In fact, it was two centuries after his death when a few quatrains appeared under his name. Many scholars doubt that he wrote so many poems and believe that many bearing a close resemblance to his philosophies, views, and prose style have been mistakenly attributed to him over the last millennia. This makes authenticating the real Khayyam poems quite difficult. In this book, I have selected 122 quatrains that in my opinion are likely genuine Khayyam poems, based on my own familiarity with Omar Khayyam's style and mindset and with Persian literature and poetic mysticism. As a bilingual author and avid reader of Persian poetry and literature, I find Fitzgerald's Rubaiyat to be an interpretation of Khayyam's poems –v. a more direct translation of the literal and mystical essence of his poems–, written in an outdated English prose (more on this in the Introduction). I believe that in this book, I have presented a more readable and accurate version.

It should be noted by the readers that the important and oft-repeated use of the concept of 'wine' and jubilance in Persian

Preface

literature –enthusiastically and literally adopted by the Victorian-era Fitzgerald in his famous work, Rubaiyat– does not signify a philosophy of pleasure-seeking in life. According to most acclaimed scholars of middle-eastern esotericism and mysticism, Khayyam and others used such code words as 'wine' and 'beloved' to make vague references to then-forbidden esoteric and alchemical philosophies and practices. To the learned 'wine and drinking wine' refer to love/light, mystical/alchemical thoughts and practices. Along with many other writers and poets of the time, Khayyam's choice in using these symbolic words was a means of communicating profound—but taboo—subjects with minimal risk of censure or persecution by the then autocratic Muslim orthodoxy. Since my own belief and lifetime of experience with Persian literature and philosophy is in accordance with such theories, I have adopted this approach to this modern translation of Khayyam's quatrain poems.

I hope I have shared a more accurate and relevant presentation of Khayyam, using a selection of his quatrain poems, with modern english readers. One that's been more understood by his Persian-speaking readers throughout the last millennia. Enjoy!

Introduction

OMAR KHAYYAM IS BELIEVED to have lived from 1048–1131 AD. Different biographers have presented him as a scholar, scientist, mathematician, astronomer, intellectual, agnostic, or mystic. All agree that he was an outstanding intellectual and scientific genius.

In the western world, Khayyam's poetry is better known than any other non-western poet. His poetry, though not his main attributed accomplishment, is also quite remarkable and inspirational.

Though the man himself remains something of an enigma.

PERSONAL LIFE

Omar Khayyam was born in 1048 in the great trading city of Nishapur in then northeastern Persia, now located in Iran.

Omar's father was Ebrahim Khayyami, a wealthy physician.

Although Omar's family were Muslims, his father seems to not have been strict about religion, even employing a mathematician by the name of Bahmanyar bin Marzban, a devotee of the ancient Persian religion of Zoroastrianism, to tutor the young Omar. Bahmanyar had been a student of the great physician, scientist, and philosopher Avicenna, and he gave Omar a thorough education in science, philosophy, and mathematics. Omar was also under the tutelage of Khawjah al-Anbari who taught him astronomy, guiding him through Ptolemy's Almagest.

In his early teens, Omar learned medical practices from his father. Khayyam also studied philosophy at Naishapur, where one

INTRODUCTION

of his fellow students wrote that he was, "... endowed with sharpness of wit and the highest natural powers."

Omar had just celebrated his eighteenth birthday in 1066, when his father Ebrahim died. A few months later his tutor Bahmanyar also died. These events marked the end of an era in Omar's life. It was time to put his family's affairs in order and move on.

In 1068, the twenty-year-old Omar Khayyam made the three month journey from Nishapur to the great city of Samarkand, a renowned center of scholarship that is now located in Uzbekistan.

In Samarkand he made contact with his father's old friend Abu Tahir, who was governor and chief judge of the city. Tahir, observing Khayyam's extraordinary talent with numbers, gave him a job in his office. Soon Khayyam was hired by the king's treasury.

Full details of Khayyam's personal life are not known. He is believed to have married and had at least one son and one daughter. Omar Khayyam died at the age of eighty three in his hometown of Nishapur on December 4, 1131. He was buried in a tomb he had personally chosen, located in a garden of flowers and trees. In 1963, the Shah of Iran had his grave exhumed and Khayyam's remains moved to a large mausoleum in Nishapur where visitors have been paying homage to the great scientist and poet to this day.

Khayyam actually published no poetry in his lifetime. Some of his musings would have potentially endangered his life. It was several years after his death, when his poems were first referenced.

HIS ERA'S POLITICAL AND HISTORICAL CONTEXT

The political events of the eleventh Century played a major role in the course of Khayyam's life. The Seljuq were a group of Turkic tribes that invaded southwestern Asia in the eleventh century AD, and eventually founded an empire that included Mesopotamia, Syria, Palestine, and most of Iran. The Seljuq empire enthusiastically adopted Islam to consolidate its power over their conquered Islamic territories. It was in this tumultuous era that Khayyam grew up.

INTRODUCTION

This was not an empire in which the learned, such as Khayyam, found life easy unless they had the support of a ruler at one of the many unstable regional courts. Khayyam himself described such difficulties of this period in the introduction to his Treatise on Demonstration of Problems of Algebra, his most famous algebra work:

> *"I was unable to devote myself to the learning of this algebra and the continued concentration upon it, because of obstacles in the vagaries of time which hindered me; for we have been deprived of all the people of knowledge save for a group, small in number, with many troubles, whose concern in life is to snatch the opportunity, when time is asleep, to devote themselves meanwhile to the investigation and perfection of a science; for the majority of people who imitate philosophers confuse the true with the false, and they do nothing but deceive and pretend knowledge, and they do not use what they know of the sciences except for base and material purposes; and if they see a certain person seeking for the right and preferring the truth, doing his best to refute the false and untrue and leaving aside hypocrisy and deceit, they make a fool of him and mock him."*

Despite the political and social challenges of his time, Khayyam was an outstanding mathematician and astronomer who wrote several works including Problems of Arithmetic, a book on music and one on algebra before he was twenty five years old.

In 1073, the Seljuq sultan, Malik-Shah, and his famous vizier, Nizam al-Mulk, invited Khayyam to go to Esfahan to establish an observatory alongside other leading astronomers. For eighteen years, Khayyam led the institution and produced works of outstanding quality. This politically calm period allowed Khayyam the opportunity to devote himself entirely to his scholarly work.

During this time Khayyam was a leading figure in compiling astronomical tables and reforming the calendar system. In 1079, under his leadership, the Jalali calendar was produced, a precise computation of time that compares with the Julian and Gregorian ones.

Khayyam also produced several works on mathematics such as the Treatise on Demonstration of Problems of Algebra, which

INTRODUCTION

contained a complete classification of cubic equations with geometric solutions found by means of intersecting conical sections. Khayyam's fame as a poet has somewhat overshadowed his many significant scientific achievements.

FITZGERALD'S TRANSLATION OF KHAYYAM, THE RUBAIYAT

What emerges from Omar's own writings, and from references to him by his contemporaries, is that he was a renowned thinker, scientist, and intellectual of his time who held very prestigious scientific offices.

Outside the world of mathematics, Khayyam is best known as a result of Edward Fitzgerald's 1859 popular translation of a collection of short four-line poems or 'quatrains', the Rubaiyat. A quatrain is a piece of verse complete in four lines. Omar's poems had attracted comparatively little attention until they inspired the Victorian-era Fitzgerald to write his celebrated The Rubaiyat of Omar Khayyam. Most often derived from Fitzgerald's translations, these quatrains have been translated into many languages, and are largely responsible for shaping European ideas about Omar Khayyam and Persian poetry in general.

Each of Omar's quatrains forms a complete poem in itself. It was Fitzgerald who conceived the idea of combining a series of these quatrains into a continuous elegy that had an intellectual unity and consistency. Fitzgerald's paraphrasing gave his translations a memorable verve and succinctness, but are considered, by some, to be excessively free translations.

The verses translated by Fitzgerald reveal a man of deep thought, troubled by the questions of the nature of reality and the eternal, the impermanence and uncertainty of life, and man's relationship to the universe. One that doubts the existence of divine providence and the afterlife, derides religious certainty, and keenly feels man's frailty and ignorance. Finding no acceptable answers to his perplexities, he chooses to put his faith instead in a celebration of the fleeting world and takes refuge in scientific and esoteric

Introduction

philosophies. Khayyam's dwelling with fundamental metaphysical questions are timelessly relevant.

Fitzgerald's Rubaiyat portrays a rather imagined Victorian figure, a somewhat romantic, hedonistic/nihilist poet, bearing little relation to the historical Omar. Fitzgerald's Rubaiyat is unfortunately often much 'spiced' with Fitzgerald's own poetic license and imagined themes and expressions. This is quite self-evident to myself and any bilingual scholars of Khayyam or others of that era and region. Fitzgerald's translations paint an imagined persona of Omar, one of mysticism, melancholy, loss of faith, anxiety about future, and unfamiliar complexity. As others tried to introduce classical figures into Victorian art, Fitzgerald also introduced a somewhat dramatized historical figure from a remote time and culture, not entirely accurately depicted.

By relying only on the original Persian version of Khayyam's poems, and using my own body of literary and linguistic knowledge, I have attempted to present Omar Khayyam in a more accurate way.

Beyond heavens' sphere is unseen,
around and about which all careen.

When your turn, be calm and sane.
Life's not a sole toil, cycles remain.

در دایره سپهر ناپیدا غور
جامی‌ست که جمله را چشانند بدور

نوبت چو به دور تو رسد آه مکن
می نوش به خوشدلی که دور است نه جور

Cosmic enigma neither you see nor I.
Secrets' spell neither you read nor I.

Much commotion flows behind a veil.
When veil falls neither you stay nor I.

اسرار اَزَل را نه تو دانی و نه من
وین حرفِ معمّا نه تو خوانی و نه من

هست از پس پرده گفت‌وگوی من و تو
چون پرده برافتد، نه تو مانی و نه من

This old court once ruled the world.
At its door many subjects curled.

Now at its ruins sits only a cuckoo,
bemusedly calling, "who, who, who."

آن قصر که با چرخ همیزد پهلو
بر درگه آن شهان نهادندی رو

دیدیم که بر کنگرهاش فاختهای
بنشسته همی گفت که کوکوکو

Friend, forsake future's worry.
Savor this mere fleeting query.

For when past this brief realm,
we'll join the timeless pilgrim.

ای دوست بیا تا غم فردا نخوریم
وین یکدم عمر را غنیمت شمریم

فردا که ازین دیر فنا درگذریم
با هفت هزار سالگان سر بسریم

Passing the 'wine-house' one night,
Saw an elder sipping a jug's sprite.

Replied to whether he feared god,
"drink, all joy and love is from light."

سرمست بمیخانه گذر کردم دوش
پیری دیدم مست وسبویی بر دوش

گفتم ز خدا شرم نداری ای پیر
گفتا کرم از خداست می نوش خموش

Born unwitting and confused,
riddles of life grew profuse.

Warily parted, yet never knowing,
logic of coming, being, or going.

اورد باضطرابم اول بوجود
جز حیرتم از حیات چیزی نفزود

رفتیم باکراه و ندانیم چه بود
زین امدن و بودن و رفتن مقصود

If the eternal crafted all of creation,
why cast it imbued with imperfection?

If perfect, why the awry transient feint?
If not, what was the eternal's intent?

دارنده چو ترکیب طبایع آراست
از بهر چه او فکندش اندر کم و کاست

گر نیک آمد شکستن از بهر چه بود
ورنیک نیامد این صور عیب کراست

Held the mouth of the wine jug,
asked it of secrets for a life long.

Thus flowed to me this advise,
"once I was you, don't surmise."

لب بر لب کوزه بردم از غایت از
تا ز او طلبم واسطه عمر دراز

با من بزبان حال میگفت این راز
عمری چو تو بوده ام دمی با من ساز

From earthen dust to celestial skies,
discovered queries of all that ties.

Solved riddles after copious ply,
except to conceive the reason why.

از جرم گل سیاه تا اوج زحل
کردم همه مشکلات کلی را حل

بگشادم بندهای مشکل به حیل
هر بند گشاده شد به جز بند اجل

Onto this old abode called earth,
day and night rise on its hearth.

It's a sanctuary to countless lovers,
and a graveyard of countless rulers.

این کهنه رباط را که عالم نام است
و آرامگه ابلق صبح و شام است

بزمی‌ست که وامانده صد جمشید است
قصریست که تکیه‌گاه صد بهرام است

Repent not from love if you love,
for penitence is another resolve.

Flowers shed, birds wail in amity.
Devotion to love is to not absolve.

توبه مکن از می اگرت می باشد
صد توبه نادمات در پی باشد

گل جامه دران و بلبلان ناله زنان
در وقت چنین توبه روا کی باشد؟

The whirling cosmos that we ponder,
minds spark with the same splendor.

Sun's the light giver, earth its bearer.
We're only viewers of all such wonder.

این چرخ فلک که ما در او حیرانیم
فانوس خیال از او مثالی دانیم

خورشید چراغ دان و عالم فانوس
ما چون صوریم کاندر او حیرانیم

Fatefully the book of youth ended,
life's spring became a dying winter.

The source of life's flow, I wonder,
whence it came, then went where?

افسوس که نامه جوانی طی شد
و آن تازه بهار زندگانی دی شد

آن مرغ طرب که نام او بود شباب
افسوس ندانم که کی آمد کی شد

Many are entranced by faith or heresy,
others fret over proof and certainty.

Echoed a faint voice from the ether,
"oh unversed, the true path is neither."

قومی متفکرند اندر ره دین
قومی به گمان فتاده در راه یقین

میترسم از آن که بانگ آید روزی
کای بیخبران راه نه آنست و نه این

Good and evil are set in man's clay.
Life's joy and sorrow cast their sway.

Deride not of the heavens' way,
its path whirls even more stray.

نیکی و بدی که در نهاد بشر است
شادی و غمی که در قضا و قدر است

با چرخ مکن حواله کاندر ره عقل
چرخ از تو هزار بار بیچارهتر است

Seek light to tame earthly urge.
With love, avarice shall purge.

Behold the elixir whose plys,
illuminates countless whys.

می خور که ز دل کثرت و قلت ببرد
و اندیشه هفتاد و دو ملت ببرد

پرهیز مکن ز کیمیایی که از او
یک جرعه خوری هزار علت ببرد

The caravan of life goes by fast.
Savour the now before it's past.

Why worry if tomorrow's aghast?
Hold love's cup, today won't last.

این قافله عمر عجب میگذرد
دریاب دمی که با طرب میگذرد

ساقی غم فردای حریفان چه خوری
پیش آر پیاله را که شب میگذرد

This clay vessel's fused with intent,
a blazing heart given as a present.

Divine potter crafts such perfection,
yet tears it to dust in recurring action.

جامی است که عقل آفرین میزندش
صد بوسه ز مهر بر جبین میزندش

این کوزهگر دهر چنین جام لطیف
میسازد و باز بر زمین میزندش

In youth we elated a brief prowess.
Gleed in the delusion of greatness.

Yet it proved only that in the end,
it was just going from soil to wind.

یک چند به کودکی باستاد شدیم
یک چند به استادی خود شاد شدیم

7

پایان سخن شنو که ما را چه رسید
از خاک در آمدیم و بر باد شدیم

Pursue light, that's a knower's realm.
Hear music, it's the prophets' psalm.

Mull not over what's past and ran.
Praise presence, that's the plan.

با باده نشین که مُلکِ محمود این است
وَزْ چنگ شنو که لحنِ داوود این است

از آمده و رفته دگر یاد مکن
حالی خوش باش ز ان که مقصود این است

The many that rose and went under,
then flew asleep in vanity's asunder.

Of their fate there is no wonder,
their words lost in aeon's thunder.

آنان که ز پیش رفته‌اند ای ساقی
در خاکِ غرور خفته‌اند ای ساقی

رو باده خور و حقیقت از من بشنو:
باد است هر آنچه گفته‌اند ای ساقی

On those days pleasant and bright,
clouds wash away the flowers' blight.

Birds merrily chant in the garden,
"beloveds, rise and face the light."

روزی‌ست خوش و هوا نه گرم است و نه سرد
ابر از رخ گلزار همی‌شوید گرد

بلبل به زبان حال خود با گل زرد
فریاد همی‌کند که می باید خورد

Our fates, life's hand puppeteers,
for truth, not need, its act steers.

A while costumed in life's clothes,
falling dormant when plays close.

ما لعبتگانیم و فلک لعبت باز
از روی حقیقت و نه از روی مجاز

بازیچه همی کنیم بر نطع وجود
افتیم بصندوق عدم یک یک باز

In the world's order feats arise,
heedless of our acts and poise.

Only good resonate with the wise.
Be good, so it's you wisdom finds.

گویند بحشر گفتگو خواهد بود
نی کار کسی بکار او خواهد بود

از خیر محض جز نکویی ناید
خوش باش که عاقبت نکو خواهد بود

When passed, wash me with light.
Sing hymns of its pure delight.

To find me on judgement day,
seek me among the ones alight.

چون درگذرم بباده شویید مرا
تلقین ز شراب ناب گویید مرا

خواهید بروز حشر یابید مرا
از خاک در میکده جویید مرا

Before facing death's plight,
navigate the path of light.

Throne's not of gold but ground.
In soil spins our merry-go-round.

زان پیش که بر سرت شبیخون آرند
فرمای که تا باده گلگون آرند

تو زر نئی ای غافل نادان که ترا
در خاک نهند و باز بیرون آرند

Sun's shining net caught the land.
Light's envoy cast its daily command.

Drink its love, salute its craft,
while truth's torch soars aloft.

خورشید کمند صبح بر بام افکند
کیخسرو روز باده در جام افکند

می خور که منادی سحرگه خیزان
آوازه «اشربوا» در ایام افکند

All comrades of the way parted,
with eternity merged, fate flaunted.

Light's path we tried to unravel.
Sooner some gained the mantle.

یاران موافق همه از دست شدند
در پای اجل یکان یکان پست شدند

خوردیم ز یک شراب در مجلس عمر
دوری دو سه پیشتر ز ما مست شدند

You, who're cast into life's crease,
bear the tries, not what you please.

For who's behind the game's throes,
only knows, only knows, only knows.

ای رفته بچوگان قضا همچون گو
چپ میخور و راست میرو و هیچ مگو

کانکس که ترا فکنده اندر تکوپو
او داند و او داند و او داند و او

With amity I was composed.
Love's ways were proposed.

Thus it gave my faint heart,
a cipher for the secret art.

چون جود ازل بود مرا انشا کرد
بر من نخست درس عشق املا کرد

وانگاه قراضه ریز قلب مرا
مفتاح در خزینه معنی کرد

Fields adorned with festive flowers,
once clutched bloodied warriors.

Flower petals fallen on soil's crust,
are reminders of beloveds lost.

در هر دشتی که لاله‌زاری بودهست
از سرخی خون شهریاری بودهست

هر شاخ بنفشه کز زمین میروید
خالی است که بر رخ نگاری بودهست

Life's choice wasn't mine to tend.
A finite journey, destined to end.

Rise friend and fill your life's cup.
With sips of love let griefs mend.

چون امدنم بمن نبد روز نخست
این رفتن بیمراد عزمیست درست

برخیز و میان ببند ای ساقی چست
کاندوه جهان بمی فرو خواهم شست

A potter's cup, crafted with care,
break it, the drinker cannot bear.

Departed's dust now joined in clay,
coalesced with love, who can tear?

ترکیب پیاله‌ای که در هم پیوست
بشکستن آن روا نمیدارد مست

چندین سر و پای نازنین از سر و دست
از مهر که پیوست و به کین که شکست

Elated bird glimpsed love's garden,
flowers' smile and flowing fountain.

Then it turned and sang in my ear,
"a life well-spent, you must endear."

چون بلبل مست راه در بستان یافت
روی گل و جام باده را خندان یافت

آمد به زبان حال در گوشم گفت
دریاب که عمر رفته را نتوان یافت

If world's craft was mine to do,
I'd redo it anew and through,

So tenets and dreams I accrue,
would be easier to construe.

گر بر فلکم دست بدی چون یزدان
برداشتمی من این فلک را ز میان

از نو فلکی دگر چنان ساختمی
کازاده بکام دل رسیدی آسان

Those versed in faith and ethics,
turned famed gurus of edicts.

None saw past night, of light's rays.
Only sang myths, fabled life's haze.

آنانکه محیط فضل و آداب شدند
در جمع کمال شمع اصحاب شدند

ره زین شب تاریک نبردند برون
گفتند فسانه‌ای و در خواب شدند

All life ends, fulfilled or naught.
Our cups filled, sweet or not.

Travelers we are, seek light.
Seas crest from storm's might.

چون عمر به سر رسد چه شیرین و چه تلخ
پیمانه چو پر شود چه بغداد و چه بلخ

می نوش که بعد از من و تو ماه بسی
از سَلخ به غُرّه آید از غره به سلخ

Of sin to virtue is just one breath,
from doubt to faith, just one breath.

Take life's breaths with content.
Destiny flees in the last breath.

از منزل کفر تا به دین یکنفس است
وز عالم شک تا بیقین یکنفس است

این یکنفس عزیز را خوش میدار
چون حاصل عمر ما همین یکنفس است

A potter's I passed a fortnight.
In dim silence sat pots in sight.

Roared one silent pot with desire,
"where's maker, seller and buyer?"

در کارگه کوزه‌گری رفتم دوش
دیدم دو هزار کوزه گویا و خموش

ناگاه یکی کوزه برآورد خروش
کو کوزه‌گر و کوزه‌خر و کوزه‌فروش

Longing for a place of peace in life,
some road trekked with less strife.

Only if after eons past on earth,
like a seed, light would spring forth.

ای کاش که جای آرمیدن بودی
یا این ره دور را رسیدن بودی

کاش از پی صد هزار سال از دل خاک
چون سبزه امید بر دمیدن بودی

Dawn's here, rise oh unbound.
Sip light's love, hymn its sound.

For those asleep journey not fore,
and those aloft descend no more.

وقت سحر است خیز ای مایه ناز
نرمک نرمک باده خور و چنگ نواز

کانها که بجایند نپایند بسی
و آنها که شدند کس نمیاید باز

The palace was once a tyrant's abode,
then gazelles birthed and foxes atoned.

That hunter who haunted thru life,
grave's peace settled all his strife.

آن قصر که جمشید در او جام گرفت
آهو بچه کرد و روبه آرام گرفت

بهرام که گور می‌گرفتی همه عمر
دیدی که چگونه گور بهرام گرفت

Where breads rise from grain seed,
and cups soothe the thirsty's need.

We dwell in such a humble throne,
that no royal gem could buy alone.

گر دست دهد ز مغز گندم نانی
وز می دو منی ز گوسفندی رانی

با لاله رخی و گوشه بستانی
عیشی بود آن نه حد هر سلطانی

To judgement day comes no wealth.
In that court no deeds stay stealth.

None returns from on high to reveal,
what waits at each turn of the wheel.

افسوس که سرمایه ز کف بیرون شد
وز دست اجل بسی جگرها خون شد

کس نامد از آن جهان که پرسم از وی
کاحوال مسافران دنیا چون شد

Cloud came and on the flowers wept.
Purified by cosmic love are the adept.

The flowers before us now are in trance.
Soon our graves will be others' stance.

ابر آمد و باز بر سر سبزه گریست
بی بادهٔ گلرنگ نمی‌باید زیست

این سبزه که امروز تماشاگه ماست
تا سبزهٔ خاک ما تماشاگه کیست

Know that you'll leave this veneer.
Behind secrets' veil you'll appear.

Doubt not, the origin stays unknown.
Angst not, for destiny is not shown.

دریاب که از روح جدا خواهی رفت
در پردهٔ اسرار فنا خواهی رفت

می نوش ندانی از کجا آمده‌ای
خوش باش ندانی به کجا خواهی رفت

Cosmic wheel's a cycle of ether.
Galaxies are rivers of purified tear.

17

Purgatory is but our pointless toils.
Heaven's alight with wisdom's spoils.

گردون نگری ز قد فرسوده ماست
جیحون اثری ز اشک پالوده ماست

دوزخ شرری ز رنج بیهوده ماست
فردوس دمی ز وقت آسوده ماست

Manifested from a divine star,
beseech love and light's altar.

Before death's fateful wind blows,
gild life's frock with wise glows.

با سرو قدی تازه‌تر از خرمن گل
از دست منه جام می و دامن گل

زان پیش که ناگه شود از باد اجل
پیراهن عمر ما چو پیراهن گل

If heart knew the secret of life,
it'd find heaven's way in death.

While here, if you learn nothing,
what'll you find when departing?

دل سر حیات اگر کماهی دانست
در مرگ هم اسرار الهی دانست

امروز که با خودی ندانستی هیچ
فردا که از خود روی چه خواهی دانست

When asleep a wise voice told,
"from daze no flowers unfold.

Union with creation is bliss,
lighten, or drift in darkness."

در خواب بدم مرا خردمندی گفت
کاز خواب کسی را گل شادی نشکفت

کاری چه کنی که با اجل باشد جفت؟
می خور که به زیر خاک می‌باید خفت

Why drudge for more possessions?
Behold life's joys, not obsessions.

Fill love's cup for it's unknown,
if a breath follows the last blown.

تا کی غم آن خورم که دارم یا نه
وین عمر به خوشدلی گذارم یا نه

پرکن قدح باده که معلومم نیست
کاین دم که فرو برم برآرم یا نه

World's here when we are gone,
neither name or relics, all alone.

Before coming, all was in order.
When gone, same will go further.

ای بس که نباشیم و جهان خواهد بود
نی نام ز ما و نی‌نشان خواهد بود

زین پیش نبودیم و نبد هیچ خلل
زین پس چو نباشیم همان خواهد بود

Moonlight pierced night's dark veil.
Fill love's cup, it's the time to avail.

Sip mindfully, for like the moon,
all shall die, then rise up soon.

مهتاب به نور دامن شب بشکافت
می نوش دمی بهتر از این نتوان یافت

خوش باش و میندیش که مهتاب بسی
اندر سر خاک یک به یک خواهد تافت

When a tree of life's limp and cut,
as decayed matter spread about.

Cast it with love in a clay lamp.
Anything comes alive once alight.

انگه که نهال عمر من کنده شود
و اجزای مرکبّم پراکنده شود

گر زانکه صُراحی کنند از گِل من
حالی که پر از باده کنی زنده شود

Reciting secrets of beloved's light,
outshines pleas or prayer to might.

You're the start and end of it all.
Set me ablaze or aloft, I've no fright.

با تو بخرابات اگر گویم راز
به زانکه بمحراب کنم بی تو نماز

ای اوّل و ای اخر خلقان همه تو
خواهی تو مرا بسوز وخواهی بنواز

Heavens' steed gallops with wings.
Pleiades and Saturn flaunt their rings.

This is a task my short life brings,
learning of them, no other things.

انروز که توسن فلک زرین کردند
و ارایش مشتری و پروین کردند

این بود نصیب ما ز دیوان قضا
ما را چه گنه قسمت ما این کردند

Pursue love, for it absolves wants,
clears mirages of dukes or counts.

Deny not that elixir from whence,
one sip will clear false pretense.

می خور که ز دل کثرت و قلت ببرد
و اندیشه هفتاد و دو ملت ببرد

پرهیز مکن ز کیمیایی که از او
یک جرعه خوری هزار علت ببرد

In passing a potter's market quay,
saw him pounding a piece of clay.

The clay pleaded with him then,
"have respect. . .I was you one day."

دی کوزه‌گری بدیدم اندر بازار
بر پاره گلی لگد همی زد بسیار

و آن گل بزبان حال با او می‌گفت
من همچو تو بوده‌ام مرا نیکودار

Through my heart said heaven,
thus of such quandaries hidden:

"Along my motion if you abscond,
it'd help free a whirling vagabond."

در گوش دلم گفت فلک پنهانی
حکمی که قضا بود ز من میدانی

در گردش خویش اگر مرا دست بدی
خود را برهاندمی ز سرگردانی

The finite span of life flees,
like water or plain's breeze.

Of two days feel no angst from,
yesterday and a day to come.

این یک دو سه روز نوبت عمر گذشت
چون آب به جویبار و چون باد به دشت

هرگز غم دو روز مرا یاد نگشت
روزی که نیامدهست و روزی که گذشت

Of higher realms, a falcon in flight,
partook a worldly descent despite.

Not finding any barer of wisdom,
it flew back with no higher insight.

بازی بودم پریده از عالم راز
بود تا که پَرم دَمی نشیبی بفراز

اینجا چو نیافتم کسی محرم راز
زان در که درامدم برون رفتم باز

Pass love's cup, my heart's aflame.
Life's fleeting, like mercury's acclaim.

Youth's blaze fades like steam,
just as wakefulness is a dream.

می در کف من نِه که دلم در تاب است
وین عمر گریزپای چون سیماب است

دریاب! که اتش جوانی اب است
خوش دار! که بیداری دولت خواب است

Grass growing beside a creek,
wavers with the caress of breeze.

Don't crush its life with ease,
it arises from dirt to appease.

هر سبزه که برکنار جویی رسته است
گویی ز لب فرشته‌خویی رسته است

پا بر سر سبزه تا به خواری ننهی
کان سبزه ز خاک لاله رویی رسته است

Khayyam, body's a transient tent,
the soul biding in a mortal convent.

Fate's builder razes that shelter,
once soul leaves, arisen further.

خیام تنت بخیمه ماند راست
سلطان روحست و منزلش دار فناست

فرّاش اجل ز بهر دیگر منزل
ویران کند این خیمه چو سلطان برخاست

Created thus of mud and fire,
light gave it life to aspire.

Regrets are lessons, a detour.
Light's way cannot be hellfire.

یزدان چون گل و جوی ما می اراست
دانست ز فعل ما چه برخواهد خاست

بی حکمش نیست هر گناهی که مراست
پس سوختن قیامت از بهر چه خواست

Heart, may you find what's true.
Find bliss upon nirvana's pew.

Love the flower's face as dew.
Then mount the sun's ray anew.

ایدل همه اسباب جهان خواسته گیر
باغ طربت به سبزه آراسته گیر

و آنگاه بر آن سبزه شبی چون شبنم
بنشسته و بامداد برخاسته گیر

Flower sighed, "golden I'm, behold,
treasures of joy for the world."

I shunned lusted wealth's dread,
for the garden's delights instead.

گل گفت که دست زرفشان اوردم
خندان خندان رو بجهان اوردم

بند از سر کیسه برگرفتم رفتم
هر نقدی بود در میان اوردم

It's said heaven is for the pious.
I think love's abode is luminous.

Behold the real, not a vague premise.
Those trusting dogmas run amiss.

گویند کسان بهشت با حور خوش است
من میگویم که آب انگور خوش است

این نقد بگیر و دست از آن نسیه بدار
کاواز دهل شنیدن از دور خوش است

My goal has been to ascertain,
script and tablet, hell or heaven.

In time did that insight depict,
heaven or hell, my actions script.

بر تو ز سپهر خاطرم روز نخست
لوح و قلم و بهشت و دوزخ میجست

پس گفت مرا معلّم از رای درست
لوح و قلم و بهشت و دوزخ با توست

They say to deny love's prose,
finds the same tomb we rose.

To seek light, beloved we are,
lest fate will be grave's repertoire.

گویند هر آن کسان که با پرهیزند
ز انسان که بمیرند چنان برخیزند

ما با می و معشوقه از آنیم مدام
باشد که به حشرمان چنان انگیزند

About earth's traits, I've learned.
Of life and death, I've learned.

Despite all that, I'm disdained,
since a mere glint I've attained.

من ظاهر نیستی و هستی دانم
من باطن هر فراز و پستی دانم

با اینهمه از دانش خود شرمم باد
گر مرتبه ای ورای مستی دانم

Rise oh light, to heart's aid go.
With radiance absolve its throe.

Rinse my dirt in your brightness,
so a purer ash in clay they throw.

بر خیز بتاب بیا ز بهر دل ما
حل کن بجمال خویشتن مشکل ما

یک کوزه شراب تا بهم نوش کنیم
ز ان پیش که کوزه ها کنند از گل ما

Tomorrow's fate none can impart.
Cherish today my restless heart.

Drink to the stars oh curious mind.
They shine but don't find our kind.

چون عهده نمی‌شود کسی فردا را
حالی خوش دار این دل پر سودا را

می نوش به ماهتاب ای ماه که ماه
بسیار بتابد و نیابد ما را

Affable is our mortal appearance,
able-statured with fair presence.

Veiled remains to our earthen raft,
the reason for such creator's craft.

هر چند که رنگ و بوی زیباست مرا
چون لاله رخ و چو سرو بالاست مرا

معلوم نشد که در طربخانه خاک
نقاش ازل بهر چه آراست مرا

Warily placed in a fragile alcove,
body, soul and mind seek love.

Of salvation or torment we'll retire,
when free of soil, wind, water, and fire.

ماییم و می و مطرب و این کنج خراب
جان و دل و جام و جامه پر درد شراب

فارغ ز امید رحمت و بیم عذاب
آزاد ز خاک و باد و از آتش و آب

Oh Earth, your flaw's deemed evil,
penchant injustice your old spell.

Yet if pierced is your dirt's heart,
an unearthly light shines out.

ای چرخ فلک خرابی از کینه
بیدادگری شیوه دیرینه تست

ای خاک اگر سینه تو بشکافند
بس گوهر قیمتی که در سینه تست

Cosmic sea flows from the unseen,
able to see its ways no one's been.

Many've composed fanciful treaties,
yet the enigma stays as mysteries.

این بحر وجود آمده بیرون ز نهفت
کس نیست که این گوهر تحقیق بسفت

هر کس سخنی از سر سودا گفتند
ز آن روی که هست کس نمی‌داند گفت

Prior times were infinite days.
Heavens turn in whirling ways.

On any dirt your foot's placed,
an elder's dust may be pressed.

پیش از من و تو لیل و نهاری بوده است
گردنده فلک نیز بکاری بوده است

هرجا که قدم نهی تو بر روی زمین
آن مردمک چشم‌نگاری بوده است

Why curse an unseen evil,
or worship a temple idol?

Who's ever witnessed hell,
or heaven and hell's spell?

تا چند زنم بروی دریاها خشت
بیزار شدم ز بت‌پرستان کنشت

خیام که گفت دوزخی خواهد بود
که رفت بدوزخ و که آمد ز بهشت

If fate's synched with your reign,
live life, though troubles remain.

Seek light, for the world's built,
only of mist, air, fire, and dirt.

ترکیب طبایع چو به کام تو دمی است
رو شاد بزی اگرچه بر تو ستمی است

با اهل خرد باش که اصل تن تو
گردی و نسیمی و غباری و دمی است

Anything solid is void inside,
only a frail shell seen and held.

All that seem are not here.
All that's unseen are there.

چون نیست ز هر چه هست جز باد بدست
چون هست بهرچه هست نقصان و شکست

انگار که هرچه هست در عالم نیست
پندار که هرچه نیست در عالم هست

The circle around which we veer,
yet no beginning or end appear.

No one knows the secret behind,
whence we come and go toward.

در دایره‌ای که آمد و رفتن ماست
او را نه بدایت نه نهایت پیداست

کس می نزند دمی در این معنی راست
کاین آمدن از کجا و رفتن بکجاست

I know not of the maker's intent,
in heaven belong, or to hell sent.

Light, music and love's presence,
exalts more than heaven's promise.

من هیچ ندانم که مرا آنکه سرشت
از اهل بهشت کرد یا دوزخ زشت

جامی و بتی و بربطی بر لب کشت
این هر سه مرا نقد و ترا نسیه بهشت

A sip of love is wiser to own,
than any kings' land or throne.

Find guidance in a wise person,
not at the pulpit or in a turban.

یک جرعه می ز ملک کاووس به است
از تخت قباد و ملکت طوس به است

هر ناله که رندی به سحرگاه زند
از طاعت زاهدان سالوس به است

The brutes that roam the land,
rile the virtuous wiser man.

Learn wisdom's poise and guile,
for pursuing the inept is futile.

اجرام که ساکنان این ایوانند
اسباب تردد خردمندانند

هان تاسر رشته خرد گم نکنی
کانان که مدبرند سرگردانند

Rigor brings freedom from craves.
Sand is pearl, once a shell braves.

Lost wealth's replaced, not spirit.
Light's eternal shining is merit.

از رنج کشیدن آدمی حر گردد
قطره چو کشد حبس صدف در گردد

گر مال نماند سر بماناد بجای
پیمانه چو شد تهی دگر پر گردد

Pursuing closely was the inevitable.
Past misdeeds stay unforgettable.

With the parting life-force I plead.
"House's failing, must leave," it decreed.

بر پشت من از زمانه تو میاید
وز من همه کار نانکو میاید

جان عزم رحیل کرد و گفتم بمرو
گفتا چکنم خانه فرو میاید

No one masters infinity's letter.
Dirt is the fate for flesh forever.

Vain one, if not in soil yet, know,
your time'll come too, don't glow.

بر چرخ فلک هیچ کسی چیر نشد
وز خوردن آدمی زمین سیر نشد

مغرور بدانی که نخورده‌ست ترا
تعجیل مکن هم بخورد دیر نشد

Facing a mirage before your eye,
lose not your way, or wonder why.

Many others've come and gone by.
Claim your stake before death's pry.

بر چشم تو عالم ارچه می‌آرایند
مگر ای بدان که عاقلان نگرایند

بسیار چو تو روند و بسیار آیند
بربای نصیب خویش کت بربایند

If fate's script isn't penned by me,
how can I account for its sanctity?

It was set before, and it'll go forward.
Hapless actors we're, without regard.

بر من قلم قضا چو بی من رانند
پس نیک و بدش ز من چرا میدانند

دی بی من و امروز چو دی بی من و تو
فردا به چه حجتم به داور خوانند

Until travelled far, destiny won't be.
Only thru heart's tears one can see.

Contend not if the heart's ablaze.
In parting from flesh, freedom waits.

تا راه قلندری نپویی نشود
رخساره بخون دل نشویی نشود

سودا چه پزی تا که چو دلسوختگان
آزاد به ترک خود نگویی نشود

Content's the one that earns bread,
a shelter to hold and a warm bed.

Neither servant, nor he's served.
Freedom's earned, then deserved.

در دهر هر آن که نیم نانی دارد
از بهر نشست آشیانی دارد

نه خادم کس بود نه مخدوم کسی
گو شاد بزی که خوش جهانی دارد

Like crops we're, sowed and reaped.
It's pointless to woe, or be seethed.

Fill love's cup and pass it fast.
We're in a history that will last.

دهقان قضا بسی چو ما کشت و درود
غم خوردن بیهوده نمیدارد سود

پر کن قدح می به کفم درنه زود
تا باز خورم که بودنیها همه بود

A life of vanity and praise,
is spent in frivolous ways.

Find light, life is a short affair,
best lived brightly and aware.

عمرت تا کی به خودپرستی گذرد
یا در پی نیستی و هستی گذرد

می نوش که عمریکه اجل در پی اوست
آن به که به خواب یا به مستی گذرد

No one finds what heaven's thrown.
None enters into bounds unknown.

Of what every expert has shown,
seems beyond them has truth flown.

کس مشکل اسرار اجل را نگشاد
کس یک قدم از دایره بیرون ننهاد

من می‌نگرم ز مبتدی تا استاد
عجز است به دست هر که از مادر زاد

Nature beholds its flowered grace,
returns the dying to its embrace.

Even clouds sapping soil's vapor,
replenish it through rainwater.

گردون ز زمین هیچ گلی برنارد
کش نشکند و هم به زمین نسپارد

گر ابر چو آب خاک را بردارد
تا حشر همه خون عزیزان بارد

While my life was spent to learn,
untold secrets began to discern.

Seventy years I tasked to thought,
to grasp that I'd revealed naught.

هرگز دل من ز علم محروم نشد
کم ماند ز اسرار که معلوم نشد

هفتاد و دو سال فکر کردم شب و روز
معلومم شد که هیچ معلوم نشد

Drops arise, then return to sea.
Dusts rejoin earth, after they flee.

What's your brief life inspired,
but a fleeting act transpired?

یک قطره آب بود با دریا شد
یک ذره خاک با زمین یکتا شد

آمد شدن تو اندرین عالم چیست
آمد مگسی پدید و ناپیدا شد

Oh heart, suffer not this old world.
Dear you're, for trivial don't scold.

All hither leave, the gone are lost.
Don't fret over what's here or not.

ای دل غم این جهان فرسوده مخور
بیهوده نئی غمان بیهوده مخور

چون بوده گذشت و نیست نابوده پدید
خوش باش غم بوده و نابوده مخور

The graved have turned to dust,
dissolved back into earth's crust.

What stupor, that until freed,
we falter over greed or creed.

این اهل قبور خاک گشتند و غبار
هر ذره ز هر ذره گرفتند کنار

آه این چه شراب است که تا روز شمار
بیخود شده و بی‌خبرند از همه کار

Who amid all that live and depart,
has returned to guidance impart?

Faced with life's crossroads, know,
that all amassed here you'll forgo.

از جمله رفتگان این راه دراز
کو باز آمده ائی که به ما گوید راز

هان بر سر این دو راهه از روی نیاز
چیزی نگذاری که نمی آئی باز

On land are the roaming asleep.
Beneath lay all that toiled the trip.

When viewing the unseen abyss,
I see only those absent or amiss.

بر مفرش خاک خفتگان می‌بینم
در زیر زمین نهفتگان می‌بینم

چندانکه به صحرای عدم مینگرم
ناآمدگان و رفتگان می‌بینم

Don't be tried with daily dismay,
though time's long or just a day.

Grant me the cup of love before,
lump of clay I'm in potters' store.

تا چند اسیر عقل هر روزه شویم
در دهر چه صد ساله چه یکروزه شویم

در ده تو بکاسه می از آن پیش که ما
در کارگه کوزه‌گران کوزه شویم

Since life's journey is brief,
being without love is mischief,

Why fret over pre life or after?
When gone, I'll ponder there.

چون نیست مقام ما در این دهر مقیم
پس بی می و معشوق خطائیست عظیم

تا کی ز قدیم و محدث امیدم و بیم
چون من رفتم جهان چه محدث چه قدیم

38

Sun doesn't sink at earth's end.
Heavens' riddle I can't portend.

Much thought taught me a lesson,
some doors are too hard to open.

خورشید به گل نهفت می‌نتوانم
و اسرار زمانه گفت می‌نتوانم

از بحر تفکرم برآورد خرد
دری که ز بیم سفت می‌نتوانم

Pundits brand me a philosopher.
Lord knows it isn't my endeavor.

But once cast in this realm's fall,
finding the true way is a vital call.

دشمن به غلط گفت که من فلسفیم
ایزد داند که آنچه او گفت نیم

لیکن چو در این غم آشیان آمده‌ام
آخر کم از آنکه من بدانم که کیم

We're the root of calm or despair,
virtue's ocean and fount of unfair.

We're low or noble, whole or sparse,
a tarnished mirror or gleaming stars.

مائیم که اصل شادی و کان غمیم
سرمایهٔ دادیم و نهاد ستمیم

39

پستیم و بلندیم و کمالیم و کمیم
آئینهٔ زنگ خورده و جام جمیم

Harping moral virtue some jaded.
With great wealth others paraded.

As their deeds seemed endowed,
the knell rang, "curtain's downed."

هر یک چندی یکی بر آید که منم
با نعمت و با سیم و زر آید که منم

چون کارک او نظام گیرد روزی
ناگه اجل از کمین بر آید که منم

I vacated this house of apathy,
leaving with only a last breath.

Rejoice only that upon my death,
light was freed from toil's dearth.

رفتم که در این منزل بیداد بُدن
در دست نخواهد بجز از باد بُدن

آن را باید به مرگ من شاد بِدن
کز دست اجل تواند آزاد بُدن

A sage was seated on barren earth,
freed of guilt, desire, heresy or faith.

With no gospel, heresy, belief or doubt,
from what source flowed such insight?

رندی دیدم نشسته بر خنگ زمین
نه کفر و نه اسلام و نه دنیا و نه دین

نه حق نه حقیقت نه شریعت نه یقین
اندر دو جهان کرا بود زهره این

An ox* flies in heavens' path.
Others decaying under earth.

Cast a thought to that satiric fact,
between them only dims protract.
(*: 'ox' refers to the Pleiades Constellation)

گاویست در آسمان و نامش پروین
یک گاو دگر نهفته در زیر زمین

چشم خردت باز کن از روی یقین
زیر و زبر دو گاو مشتی خر بین

Tending to the enlightened trial,
bests the worship of a false idol,

If love's smitten are bound for hell,
then heaven is a deserted spell.

می خوردن و گرد نیکوان گردیدن
به زانکه بزرق زاهدی ورزیدن

گر عاشق و مست دوزخی خواهد بود
پس روی بهشت کس نخواهد دیدن

Once soul leaves its mortal shell,
that corpse joins earth's mantle.

Someday, for another's last spell,
its dust may be their grave's fill.

از تن چو برفت جان پاک من و تو
خشتی بنهند بر مغاک من و تو

وانگه ز برای خشت گور دگران
در کالبدی کشند خاک من و تو

Worldly wares that sustain needs,
justify all your efforts and deeds.

Excess wealth's petty to the wise.
So don't squander life's real prize.

آن مایه ز دنیا که خوری یا پوشی
معذوری اگر در طلبش میکوشی

باقی همه را یگان نیرزد هشدار
تا عمر گرانبها بدان نفروشی

Springs return and winters pass.
Time drops down life's hourglass.

Immerse in light, not sorrows.
Grief's poison, but love hallows.

از آمدن بهار و از رفتن دی
اوراق وجود ما همی گردد طی

می خور! مخور اندوه که فرمود حکیم
غمهای جهان چو زهر و تریاقش می

A pot I brought from the bazar,
whispered secrets of lands afar:

"A king I was once, on a golden throne,
but clay now, with deeds to atone."

از کوزه‌گری کوزه خریدم باری
آن کوزه سخن گفت ز هر اسراری

شاهی بودم که جام زرینم بود
اکنون شده‌ام کوزه هر خماری

On hope's tree may I find crop.
Along secrets' rope, a way up.

Freed from prison of lone carcass,
find a path to the eternal endless.

بر شاخ امید اگر بری یافتمی
هم رشته خویش را سری یافتمی

تا چند ز تنگنای زندان وجود
ای کاش سوی عدم دری یافتمی

Hampered by senses and parts,
we confront the trials of hearts.

We're soil that see bright lights.
We're air that hear sirens' rites.

تا چند حدیث پنج و چار ای ساقی
مشکل چه یکی چه صد هزار ای ساقی

خاکیم همه چنگ بساز ای ساقی
بادیم همه باده بیار ای ساقی

Wherever I glance, I see in sight,
sublime flora fed by flows of light.

Earth is paradise, it's not dreamt.
Eden's here, we need not repent.

چندان که نگاه می‌کنم هر سویی
از سبزه بهشت است وز کوثر جویی

صحرا چو بهشت است ز کوثر کم گوی
بنشین به بهشت با بهشتی رویی

Passing the potter's one night,
saw the master's usual sight.

Crafting clay pots without vaunt,
of beggars' crud and kings' flaunt.

در کارگه کوزه‌گری کردم رای
در پایه چرخ دیدم استاد بپای

می‌کرد دلیر کوزه را دسته و سر
از کله پادشاه و از دست گدای

If worldly ways came from wisdom,
all would be in balance and rhythm.

If its affairs were guided by justice,
the humble need not bear malice.

گر کار فلک به داد سنجیده بُدی
احوال فلک جمله پسندیده بُدی

ور عدل بُدی به کارها در گردون
کی خاطر اهل فضل رنجیده بُدی

Heart heard a cosmic thunder:

"Astral laws do I set, you ponder?
If I swayed my own path yonder,
I'd be free from such wander."

در گوش دلم گفت فلک پنهانی
حکمی که بُود قضا ز من میدانی؟

در گردش خویش اگر مرا دست بُدی
خود را برهاندمی ز سرگردانی

CPSIA information can be obtained
at www.ICGtesting.com
Printed in the USA
BVHW051006090821
613981BV00002B/111